Class 47s
The Jack of All Trades

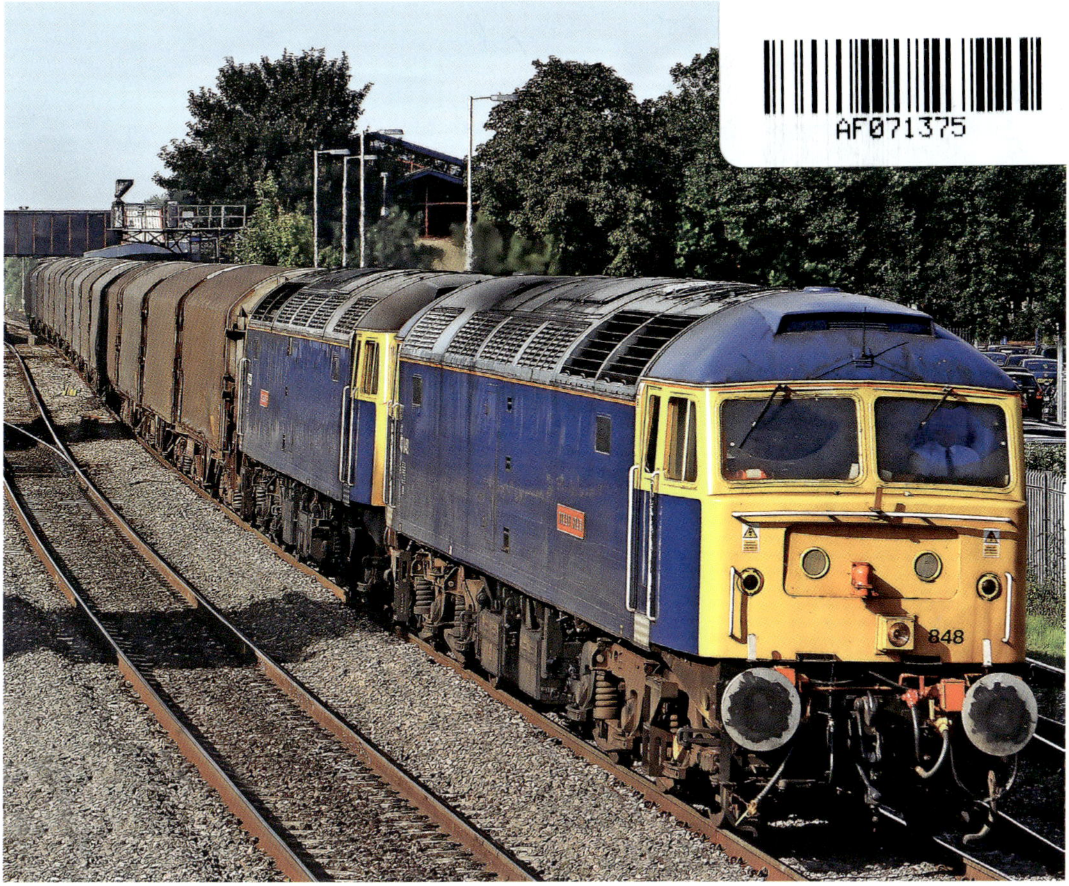

MARK V. PIKE

Key Books

BRITAIN'S RAILWAYS SERIES, VOLUME 45

Front cover image: This is Newton Abbot, where we see 47711 *County of Hertfordshire* departing with a westbound Virgin Cross Country service. To the right is 47792 *Saint Cuthbert*, which had arrived with a railtour. This was a day of celebrations in conjunction with the Festival of Transport being held over this weekend, which also explains the amount of people milling around! 13 May 2000.

Back cover image: Upon transfer south from Scotland, 47705 (formerly *Lothian*) was an early recipient of Network SouthEast livery. Soon after this repaint, it is seen arriving at Exeter St Davids with 1B05, the 08.45 London Paddington to Penzance service. 5 August 1989.

Title page image: This is 47848 *Titan Star* + 47805 *Talisman* powering south through Oxford station with 6Z48, the 13.05 Burton West Yard to Dollands Moor empty steel train. 10 September 2009.

Contents page image: This is the naming ceremony of Colas Rail 47739 *Robin of Templecombe*, being held in the one remaining siding of the once massive yard at Templecombe station. It is being named by the man himself, Robin Gould. At that time, he was the only person still on active railway service to have worked on the legendary Somerset & Dorset Railway. The whole ceremony was a complete surprise to Robin, who was absolutely delighted! He finally retired in 2009, but sadly passed away in 2013. The nameplates were, however, transferred to Colas Rail 56049, as the Class 47 now operates with GB Railfreight (GBRf). 30 September 2008.

Published by Key Books
An imprint of Key Publishing Ltd
PO Box 100
Stamford
Lincs PE9 1XQ

www.keypublishing.com

The right of Mark V. Pike to be identified as the author of this book has been asserted in accordance with the Copyright, Designs and Patents Act 1988 Sections 77 and 78.

Copyright © Mark V. Pike, 2023

ISBN 978 1 80282 356 1

All rights reserved. Reproduction in whole or in part in any form whatsoever or by any means is strictly prohibited without the prior permission of the Publisher.

Typeset by SJmagic DESIGN SERVICES, India.

Contents

Introduction 4

Chapter 1   BR Days 1985–1999 5

Chapter 2   From 2000 to the Present Day 41

Chapter 3   Open Days and Heritage Lines 82

Introduction

Plans for the Class 47 locomotives had been developed as a follow-on from the Class 44–46 'Peak' locomotives already in service and as a development of prototype locomotive D0260 *Lion* and D0280 *Falcon*. As a result of research and testing of these prototypes, the construction of the first of the Class 47 began in 1962. Totalling 512 locomotives, this huge order was placed between three construction works: Brush Works at Loughborough, Crewe (British Rail Engineering LTD (BREL)) and Gorton (Beyer Peacock). These were tasked with assembling 310, 182 and 20 locomotives respectively. Unfortunately, Beyer Peacock was struggling at the time, so much so that BREL agreed to assume responsibility for its order (D1842–D1861) and BREL's Gorton Foundry closed in 1966. The full order of 512 was eventually completed in 1968, by which time two locomotives had already been scrapped due to serious mishaps. There were various differences in the technical elements of the locos, especially with the initial batch of 20 (D1500–D1520). Five locomotives (D1702–D1706) were also fitted with a Sulzer experimental engine designated 12LVA24, while the rest of the fleet were equipped with the standard Sulzer 12LDA28C engine. These five examples were different enough to be designated as Class 48. By 1971, however, the locomotives had been converted to the standard Brush Type 4 classification, with the standard power plant. The total now stood at 508 active locomotives, as four had been scrapped as a result of serious accidents.

The locomotives went on to serve British Rail (BR) very well indeed, turning their hand to every sort of train type across the UK, and it wasn't until 1986 that things started to change. With spares becoming an issue and the introduction of new trains that took some of their work away, inroads started being made. It was pretty obvious that the first locomotives to be taken out of service would be the non-standard first batch of 20, now numbered 47401 to 47420. Three examples were deemed as life-expired in February 1986 and withdrawn. The remainder of this batch was culled over the next two years, based on how recently they had received overhauls. All 20 were withdrawn by 1992. It then took almost another 20 years until the last Freightliner locomotives were withdrawn.

However, with such a versatile locomotive, many initially ended up in storage rather than being scrapped straight away, and as a result have survived into preservation. Indeed, many are still active on the UK network to this day with various operating companies.

This is 47245 *The Institute of Export* stabled between duties at Swindon. 23 March 1995.

Chapter 1
BR Days 1985–1999

We start this book with a couple of images of a typical passenger train formation to be seen during the 1980s. 47473 passes Sprey Point near Teignmouth with an unidentified eastbound service. After many more years of service, this loco was scrapped in early 1998. June 1985.

Heading in the opposite direction at the same location is an equally typical formation headed by 47478, which is sporting a silver roof from a recent spell based at Stratford Depot. This loco was scrapped during 2006. June 1985.

A few years later, and things had started to move on from plain BR blue. This is 47406 (formerly *Rail Riders*) awaiting departure from Exeter St Davids with 1E36, the 11.17 Penzance to Newcastle service. Unusually, this loco was based at Immingham at this time. It was scrapped in 1995 with the name transferring to 47488. 30 July 1988.

The rudimentary passenger facilities at Bruton station, Somerset, are passed by BR blue 47557 powering west with 1C17, the 08.17 London Paddington to Paignton service. In recent years, this station has become a little more used but is still rather quiet, and still with meagre facilities! At the time, this loco was based at Bristol Bath Road and was later to become 47721 *Saint Bede*. It was scrapped in mid-2007. 17 September 1988.

47500 *Great Western* was one of a few locos painted in green livery during 1985 for the GWR 150 celebrations. It is seen arriving at Exeter St Davids with a service bound for Plymouth. The loco was to survive in a later guise as 47770 *Reserved* from the mid-1990s, until it was secured for preservation in 2007. However, this was not to last; the loco was renumbered back to 47500 and saw a short spell of service with West Coast Railway Company (WCRC) until its withdrawal after suffering a serious fire in 2013. It was finally cut up in 2020. 3 August 1985.

Still at Exeter St Davids, this is 47457 *Gazelle*, arriving with 1C17, the 08.17 London Paddington to Paignton service. This loco was one of many examples at the time to carry an unofficial name and was originally named *Ben Line*. It was scrapped in 1997. 24 August 1991.

Our last view at Exeter St Davids sees 'large logo' 47805 attached to a West Coast Main Line (WCML) coaching set, complete with Driving Van Trailer (DVT) 82104 behind the loco, working 1V48, the 10.25 Liverpool Lime Street to Paignton. During this period, a WCML set of coaches was regularly used on a summer Saturday to cope with passenger demand. 47805 can still be seen on the main line today, back in two-tone green livery and working for Locomotive Services Limited (LSL). 5 August 1989.

Back in the days of inter-regional services to the south coast resort of Weymouth, this is 47662 passing Winfrith (between Wool and Moreton) with 1O09, the 08.18 Manchester Piccadilly to Weymouth service. At this time, the loco was allocated to Bristol Bath Road depot and was only a couple of months away from being renumbered as 47817. It worked in this guise until 2003, when it was totally rebuilt as 57311. At the time of writing, in late 2022, it is stored at Eastleigh Works pending further developments. 9 September 1989.

Heading in the opposite direction at Winfrith on the same day as the previous image, we see 47485 with 1M32, the 10.00 Weymouth to Manchester Piccadilly, passing beneath Broomhill Road bridge. This loco was allocated to Crewe Diesel Depot at the time and was scrapped during 1997. 9 September 1989.

It was quite unusual to see one of the original 20 (D1500–D1520) of the class on passenger trains in the south during the late 1980s when moves were already being made to withdraw them from service. During the summer months, however, when many extra trains ran, loco availability became very short at times. This is 47407 (formerly *Aycliffe*) approaching Broomhill Bridge at Winfrith with 1M20, the 15.25 Weymouth to Liverpool Lime Street service, which it worked to Birmingham New Street. The loco was withdrawn from service around 18 months after the date of this image and scrapped during 1995. 9 September 1989.

The first of three images taken during my time on the permanent way department at Bournemouth. This is 47457 *Ben Line* arriving at Bournemouth Central with 1S39, the 08.34 Poole to Glasgow Central service ('The Wessex Scot'). This loco later went on to feature in some of the last London Paddington to Newbury/Oxford services in the early 1990s. 17 February 1988.

A view from the long-demolished Branksome signal box as 47635, complete with a Highland Terrier on the bodyside negotiates its way out of the lines leading to/from Bournemouth Traction and Rolling Stock Maintenance Depot (TRSMD) with the empty coaching stock (ECS) for the 'Wessex Scot', which is heading a few miles down the line to Poole. These two lines that now lead to the depot were once part of the main line used by services arriving and departing from the former Somerset & Dorset Railway to Bath and terminating at Bournemouth West, which was about a mile from this location. Unfortunately, both the Somerset & Dorset line and the terminus at Bournemouth West were closed back in the late 1960s. Thankfully, the loco has fared rather better. Allocated the number D1606 from new, then 47029 under Total Operations Processing System (TOPS), it spent its first 20 years or so on BR Western Region before it was transferred to Scotland in January 1986, the same time as it gained Electric Train Heating (ETH) and its present number. After about four years north of the border, it came back south to Crewe but was withdrawn from service during 2004. In 2007, however, it was saved for preservation and did a short spell on the Swanage Railway until moving to its present home at the Epping Ongar Railway. See also pages 92/93. 5 November 1986.

Also viewed from Branksome signal box, this was a very rare sight at the time. 33112 *Templecombe*, propelling a 4-TC unit on a Weymouth to London Waterloo service, had failed between Wareham and Poole and the only loco in the vicinity was 47215, which was commandeered to couple up to the rear and push the ensemble to Bournemouth, where the 33 would have been removed in any case. This arrangement was not as easy as it sounds, as it required a driver to be in the Class 47 cab closest to the 33, with a person in the rear of the TC unit directing the very slow-travelling proceedings. I have my doubts this sort of manoeuvre would be allowed today. 17 February 1988.

We are now a few miles further west at Wareham as 'large logo' 47591 arrives with 1E41, the 09.10 Weymouth to Newcastle service. Since this date, the loco has undergone a few renumberings and has carried a couple of names, but it is still in service on the main line as 47804, operating with WCRC. 26 May 1988.

Still at Wareham but this time a view from the signal box as 47582 *County of Norfolk* slows for the station stop with 1O11, the 10.15 Liverpool Lime Street to Weymouth service. This is another loco that underwent a few identity and name changes but was probably best known when it wore Network SouthEast livery during the early 1990s. It was scrapped in 2008. 5 September 1992.

It seems unthinkable these days, but up until the 1990s relief trains were often run to cope with passenger demand, mainly through the summer months. Probably mustered up at short notice, this is ex-works Railfreight grey-liveried 47285 racing through Holton Heath station with 1Z21, the 09.40 Crewe to Weymouth relief. The loco had rather an uneventful life, at this time being based at Bristol Bath Road. It was withdrawn in the mid-1990s and finally scrapped in 2005. 6 September 1986.

Moving to Maiden Newton on the Castle Cary to Weymouth line, we see 'Inter-City' main line-liveried 47566 arriving with the 15.49 Bristol Temple Meads to Weymouth service. This is another loco that led a pretty uneventful life. It was scrapped during 2006. 9 September 1989.

A month before, at the same location as the previous image, this is 47971 *Robin Hood*, waiting to depart northbound this time, with the 11.06 Weymouth to Bristol Temple Meads ECS. This was the day of the annual Weymouth carnival, which was bolstered by the visit of the Radio 1 Roadshow, and thus quite a few extra trains were run to meet passenger numbers heading to the seaside resort. The loco itself (formerly 47480) was interesting, as it was renumbered as 97480 for about a year in 1988, but then to 47971 in 1989 until it was scrapped in 2001. Locos 47971–47976 were numbered as such by Derby RTC for (theoretically) test train-only use. On this occasion, it was in passenger service, presumably as no other loco was available. 19 August 1992.

This time we see a very smart-looking 47741 *Resilient* in the bright red Rail Express Systems (RES) livery, arriving at Weymouth with the Yeovil to Weymouth non-steam section of a charter hauled by 35028 *Clan Line*. This loco (formerly 47597) was withdrawn in the early 2000s and scrapped in 2008. 15 October 1994.

The first of a few shots in the Westbury area now, as 'large logo' 47540 arrives at Westbury station with the Fridays-only 1B10, the 15.30 London Paddington to Plymouth service. This was another example set aside to supposedly work test trains only, firstly gaining the number/name 47975 *The Institution of Civil Engineers* in 1990, then reverting to 47540 after about five years but retaining its name. It can class itself a little unlucky in later life, as it was initially saved for preservation in the early 2000s, but after many more years in open storage it was finally scrapped during 2016. Circa 1989.

A misty morning this time sees 'celebrity' GWR green 47484 *Isambard Kingdom Brunel* at Upton Scudamore, between Warminster and Westbury, unusually leading a Portsmouth Harbour to Cardiff Central service. At this time, the vast majority of these services were in the hands of Class 33 locos. This 47 was withdrawn from service during early 2002 but later secured for preservation. It is now owned by the Pioneer Preservation Group, but is still in storage at Wishaw awaiting developments at the time of writing. 5 April 1988.

About two miles as the crow flies from the location seen in the previous image, we see 47484 *Isambard Kingdom Brunel* again, this time speeding west along the Westbury avoiding line with a London Paddington to Penzance service. 14 September 1990.

A year earlier than the last shot, we see 47817 at the same point with the same London Paddington to Penzance service, but somewhat shorter this time! This loco had just been renumbered from 47662 and went on to work for many years on cross-country services. In early 2003, it was completely rebuilt, becoming 57311, and as such is currently in storage at Eastleigh Works awaiting developments. 1 September 1989.

Approaching Westbury station is 'large logo'-liveried 47447 with an unidentified service from the West of England to London Paddington. This loco was scrapped during 1994. 1 September 1989.

Once again at the same spot, but this time on the same day as the last image, this is 47825 *Thomas Telford*, approaching with the 08.20 Exeter St Davids to London Paddington service. This loco has had a somewhat eventful life in later years. It was withdrawn from service in the early 2000s but was chosen as the test bed for the upcoming Class 57 project, becoming 57601 in a striking purple livery (with the nickname 'Purple Ronnie'!) during 2001. A few years later, First Great Western (FGW) ordered 57602–57605 for use on their sleeper services. This loco, however, is still in service in 2022; now operating with WCRC in 'Northern Belle' Pullman livery, it sees regular main line charter work. 1 September 1989.

Further west we see 'Inter-City'-liveried 47611 *Thames* at Plymouth station with the stock for 1A85, the 15.50 service to London Paddington. The loco became 47837 soon after the date of this image, but due to fire damage in 1992 it was withdrawn very early in comparison to the other Class 478XX locos, and scrapped soon after in 1993. 14 July 1989.

Class 47s: The Jack of All Trades

On the same day at Plymouth, this is 47574 *Benjamin Gimbert GC* awaiting departure with a Penzance to London Paddington service. At this time, the loco was allocated for a brief spell at Bristol Bath Road depot (BR). The name on this loco was previously carried by 47577 and was later revived on 66077, which still carries it to this day. 47574, however, was scrapped during 2005. 14 July 1989.

Summer Saturdays in the past could often produce some unexpected locos working passenger trains, as the running of many extra holiday trains around the country stretched motive power availability. This is Railfreight 'red stripe'-liveried 47363 *Billingham Enterprise* arriving at Bristol Temple Meads with the 09.18 Manchester Piccadilly to Paignton service. A few people obviously appreciated the haulage by a member of the class usually dedicated to freight trains! The loco was withdrawn from service during 2000 but was not scrapped until 2010. 29 June 1991.

A few years earlier, at Bristol Temple Meads, this is 'large logo' 47424 arriving with 1M45, the 11.33 Penzance to Liverpool Lime Street service. After a non-eventful life, the loco was scrapped in early 1994. 29 August 1987.

Also at Bristol Temple Meads, 47143 on the left is seen waiting to depart for Cardiff Central on a service from Portsmouth Harbour, whilst to the right is 47481, awaiting departure with a train to the North of England. 47143 was scrapped during 1994, and 47481 met its fate during 2003. *Circa* 1987.

Making a terrific sight as it rounds the curve on the approach to Starcross station is 47451, with an unidentified train bound for the West Country. Over the intervening 36 years, this location has, somewhat unbelievably, become totally overgrown by bushes. The loco was scrapped in early 1994. June 1986.

Looking in the opposite direction at the same location as the previous image, we see 47564 with an unidentified eastbound service from the West Country. This loco later became 47761 and was withdrawn during 2003, but was later saved for preservation. However, it is still stored in 2022 and used as a source of spare parts for other preserved examples at the Midland Railway Centre. June 1986.

Class 47s: The Jack of All Trades

Having just passed through Teignmouth station, 'large logo' 47651 is about to start its passage along the famous sea wall whilst in charge of an unidentified express bound for the North of England. Later becoming 47806, and later still 57309 after a complete rebuild, it is currently in service with Direct Rail Services (DRS), being mainly used for 'Thunderbird' duties on the WCML. 29 June 1986.

To Scotland now, where we see an absolutely filthy 47492 *The Enterprising Scot* in 'Inter-City' livery stabled on Inverness depot. This loco was withdrawn in 2002 but was later taken on by WCRC located at Carnforth; it has not worked since, however, and was probably just used as a source of spares. 1 March 1990.

This is 47677 *University of Stirling* arriving at Perth station with an Edinburgh to Inverness service. Formerly numbered 47617, this was one of seven examples converted to 47/6s and fitted with high-phosphorus brake blocks and also a higher electric train-heating supply rating for dedicated use on Scottish sleeper services. All seven of these locos were based at Inverness. This particular loco was withdrawn in early 1998 and scrapped very soon after. 26 August 1992.

Moving to Edinburgh Waverley, we see ScotRail 'blue stripe' 47715 approaching with a push-pull service from Glasgow Central. This loco had been converted from 47502 just four months prior to this view and was named *Haymarket* the following month. After working the push-pull services for a couple of years, it became surplus as new stock was introduced, so was transferred south to Old Oak Common in mid-1990. Fortunately, the loco still survives to this day on the Wensleydale Railway in full working order. 19 July 1985.

This is 47708 *Waverley* approaching Dundee with an unidentified service formed of a mixture of 'Inter-City' and ScotRail-liveried coaches. Converted from the former 47516, this was another loco that moved south during 1990 to Old Oak Common, where it gained the name *Templecombe* until its withdrawal. It was scrapped during 1995. 1 March 1990.

Our last view north of the border sees 47710 *Sir Walter Scott* having just drawn to a halt at Aberdeen with a service from Glasgow Central. Converted from 47496, this one also moved south when no longer required by ScotRail and later became *Capital Radio's Help A London Child*, again working off Old Oak Common. Later still, it became *Quasimodo*, then *Lady Godiva* when it was operated by the now defunct Fragonset Railways. It was scrapped in 2007. 1 March 1990.

When the former ScotRail push-pull 47/7s were sent south, a few entered service almost immediately, working various trains on the Western Region based on Old Oak Common, and this brought about the sight of ScotRail-liveried locos combined with Network SouthEast stock. This is 47711 *Greyfriars Bobby* at Reading with an Oxford to London Paddington service. Only the ScotRail wording had been removed at this point, but the nameplates were to be removed a month after this picture was taken. It did eventually receive Network SouthEast livery and then later Virgin Cross Country red colours when it later went on to operate with Virgin Cross Country. It was eventually scrapped during 2004. 14 November 1990.

BR Days 1985–1999

One loco that never received Network SouthEast livery was 47706 (formerly *Strathclyde*), which soldiered on in the south to the end of its days in very worn ScotRail colours. It is seen here about to depart Basingstoke with a London Waterloo to Exeter St Davids service. Note the Network SouthEast logo on the cab side. It was scrapped during 1995. 10 July 1992.

Recently repainted into Network SouthEast livery, this is 47701 *Old Oak Common Traction & Rolling Stock Depot*, just arrived at Eastleigh with an ECS working from Salisbury to Eastleigh Depot. After going on to work with Fragonset, this loco was withdrawn in the early 2000s but was later saved for preservation. It is currently in operational condition at the Nemesis Rail site at Burton-on-Trent. 29 October 1991.

Class 47s: The Jack of All Trades

One of the first examples to be released by ScotRail during 1989 was 47705 (formerly *Lothian*), which became an early recipient of Network SouthEast livery. It is seen here, soon after this repaint, arriving at Exeter St Davids with 1B05, the 08.45 London Paddington to Penzance service. After its stint with Network SouthEast came to an end in the early 1990s, it was taken on by the short-lived Waterman Railways until, in 2003, it was completely rebuilt into 57303. Although it is now under the ownership of DRS, it is currently stored out of service. 5 August 1989.

This time we see 47707 *Holyrood* arriving at London Paddington with a train from Oxford. Unusually, the Scottish-themed name was retained on this loco upon transfer south, but I think the reason for this was the fact that rather than being bolted on, the plates were actually welded on! The loco lingered on for almost ten years until it was scrapped during 2010. 4 May 1991.

BR Days 1985–1999

Powering around the Didcot station avoiding line, this is 47579 *James Nightall GC* with a London Paddington to Oxford service. This loco went on to become 47793 *Saint Augustine* when operating for English, Scottish & Welsh Railway (EWS), later still becoming *Christopher Wren*, but it was withdrawn during the mid-2000s. In 2007, however, it was saved for preservation and can presently be found in fully operational condition on the Mid-Hants Railway, having reverted to its identity of 47579. 26 July 1991.

To the City of Oxford now, as 47576 *Kings Lynn* has just arrived with a terminating train from London Paddington. This loco was withdrawn during 2003. *Circa* 1990.

Oxford is again the location as we see Glasgow Eastfield-allocated 'large logo'-liveried 47633 awaiting departure with 1E40, the 09.17 London Paddington to York which the loco worked to Birmingham New Street. Before its renumbering and fitting with ETH, this loco was 47083 *Orion*, one of the original named Western Region locos. It was scrapped during 1994. 7 July 1990.

We are now 'on the blocks' at the former Southern Railway terminus at London Waterloo, where Network SouthEast-liveried 47530 has just arrived with a service from Exeter St Davids. At the time, this loco was more often seen working the London Paddington to Oxford/Newbury services. It was scrapped in early 2001. 10 April 1991.

Moving over to Reading for a few shots, we see a very smart Network SouthEast-liveried 47547 *University of Oxford* arriving with an Oxford to London Paddington train. Despite being withdrawn during 1998, it was not actually scrapped until 2005. 4 May 1991.

An even smarter 47579 *James Nightall GC* is seen again as it arrives at Reading with a London Paddington to Newbury service. At this time, the loco had just been transferred to Old Oak Common depot from Stratford. May 1990.

Right: Here we see the arrival of 47364+47521 with an Oxford to London Paddington service. Train loco 47521 had failed en route, and the freight-only 47/3 was scrambled to rescue it. 47521 was scrapped in 1995 but 47364 fared somewhat better, lasting until scrapping in 2000. 27 February 1992.

Below: Our final view at Reading sees 47431 *Silurian* arriving with a London Paddington to Oxford train. The name on this loco was one of a number of unofficial names applied to various locos around this time. It was withdrawn from service just two months after the date of this shot and scrapped during 1997. 18 June 1992.

Now, a series of shots taken at Salisbury of various locos working West of England services. This is 47702 *Saint Cuthbert* arriving with a terminating service from London Waterloo. This loco later went on to do a spell with Virgin Cross Country and was renamed *County of Suffolk*. 17 March 1993.

On the same day as the previous shot, the loco has run round its train and is now waiting to depart platform 3 with the 12.13 service to London Waterloo. The loco was eventually withdrawn in 2000 and scrapped during 2005. 17 March 1993.

This is the scene at the western end of the station as Parcels Sector-liveried 47712 *Lady Diana Spencer* has just arrived at platform 3 with a terminating service from London Waterloo, whilst to the right 47705 has just drawn to a halt with a London Waterloo to Exeter St Davids service. It is good to see the driver of 47712 happy in his work! Both of these locos are still with us today; 47705, however, was rebuilt in 2003 after doing a spell with Waterman Railways to become 57303, whilst 47712 is owned by the Crewe Diesel Preservation Group (on short-term hire to LSL), currently back in ScotRail livery and fully main line registered. 20 September 1991.

Towards the end of loco haulage on Waterloo to Exeter services, a number of different locos put in an appearance. Another Parcels Sector-liveried loco, this time 47535 *University of Leicester*, is seen departing platform 2 with an Exeter St Davids to London Waterloo service. It has always been a tricky start from this platform, due to the severe curvature of the track and a slight rising gradient. This loco was scrapped during 2004. 17 April 1993.

Another Exeter St Davids to London Waterloo service is just preparing to depart platform 2, this time behind 47579 *James Nightall GC*. Formerly allocated to Stratford Depot in East London to work London Liverpool Street to Norwich services, this loco was moved to Old Oak Common in mid-1990. It can currently be found in service on the Mid-Hants Railway. 22 March 1991.

This is 47707 *Holyrood* arriving at platform 3 with 1V11, the 10.55 London Waterloo to Exeter St Davids service. Note the scaffolding on the track in platform 4; this was a Sunday, and the engineers had possession of the platform for canopy work. The loco was scrapped during 2010. 15 November 1992.

Back at the eastern end of the station now, as 47708 *Templecombe* gets to grips with 1O35, the 09.28 Exeter St Davids to London Waterloo service. The crowds of people on the station in the background were mostly there for a couple of steam charters operating on this day. Formerly named *Waverley* when operating with ScotRail, this loco was quite an early casualty, being scrapped in 1995. 28 June 1992.

Also nearing the end of loco-hauled services, this is 47704 in Rail Express Systems (RES) livery waiting to depart platform 3 with the 15.13 service to London Waterloo. Formerly *Dunedin* when operating with ScotRail, this loco was a relatively late addition to the West of England line compared to the other 47/7s, being moved south to Crewe Diesel Depot to join the Parcels Sector in late 1991. It was still allocated there when this shot was taken, but was scrapped during 2006. 24 February 1993.

Another of the Parcels Sector red-liveried examples was 47703 *The Queen Mother*, seen here waiting to depart from platform 4 with 1L10, the 12.15 Salisbury to London Waterloo. Formerly *Saint Mungo* when operating with ScotRail, it later worked for Fragonset as *Hermes*, but was put into storage during 2007. After a spell in preservation at the Wensleydale Railway, it is now located at Doncaster Works in a semi-preserved state with an unknown future ahead of it. 19 February 1993.

Left: Moving away from Salisbury now, we see 47707 *Holyrood* again, this time arriving at Wareham hauling a perfectly uniform rake of Network SouthEast Mk1 coaches as 2V76, the 10.20 Weymouth to Swansea service. This was a Saturdays-only train, unusually routed via Wareham/Southampton rather than direct via Yeovil/Westbury. 1 September 1990.

Below: 47703 *The Queen Mother* is seen again, this time drawing into Sherborne with an Exeter St Davids to London Waterloo service. 10 April 1993.

This is 47811, unusually arriving at Southampton Central platform 3 with a northbound Cross-Country service. After operating for many years after this date with FGW, the loco was later taken on to Freightliner's books, but it rarely moved from Crewe Basford Hall yard and gradually fell into a state of disrepair. It was finally scrapped in November 2022, just prior to these words being written. 10 April 1991.

We have now reached Basingstoke to see 47583 *County of Hertfordshire* arriving from the west with a service bound for London Waterloo. Some readers may remember the unique version of 'large logo' livery carried by this loco back in 1981 to celebrate the Royal Wedding of Prince Charles and Lady Diana Spencer. It later went on to work for RES as 47734 *Crewe Diesel Depot* but was finally scrapped during 2008. 10 July 1992.

A couple of images showing 47s with the Royal Train. A bit of a mystery here, though. This is 47484 *Isambard Kingdom Brunel* during a shunt operation at Newton Abbot. I have lost all my notes for this and have no idea what was going on, or the reason for the train being there! However, the tracks that the train was standing on and the platform in view were taken out of use in mid-1987. The loco was withdrawn from service during 2000 but later preserved, although at the time of writing it has never been restored and is now in quite a decayed state. *Circa* 1986.

A few years later, we see immaculate 47834 *Fire Fly* approaching Poole with an ECS working from Weymouth. Later in its life, this loco became 47798 *Prince Henry* and was dedicated (almost) to Royal Train duties until preservation in 2004. 20 November 1991.

The popular photographic location of Lambert's Bridge, which carries a minor road over the line just west of Westbury, is the viewpoint now as we see 47204 approaching with a short stone train that probably originated at Whatley Quarry and is now heading for Westbury Yard. In later years, this loco was briefly renumbered 47388 before reverting to 47204 a short while after. In mid-2000, however, it was completely rebuilt to become 57012. It is still operational to this day with WCRC. 24 February 1987.

A few years later and viewed from the same bridge but looking in the opposite direction, we see Railfreight Construction-liveried 47063 heading west out of Westbury with a trip working to one of the Somerset quarries. Note the four-wheeled stone wagons, now long since gone. This loco was allocated to Cardiff Canton at this time but was just a couple of months away from transfer north to Glasgow Eastfield. It survived until scrapping came in 1996. 14 September 1990.

Right: Thirty-odd years ago, loco convoys were not as common as they are today. This is, however, 47050+47320+47187 passing through Burton-on-Trent on their way north to an unknown destination, possibly Toton Depot. Of these locos, 47050 and 47320 were scrapped in 1996 and 47187 was completely rebuilt during 1998 to become 57006, which is currently with WCRC, stored at Carnforth out of service. 26 February 1992.

Below: Freight trains don't come much shorter than this! 47201 is captured heading south at Stafford hauling just one wagon. This loco was scrapped during 2007. 22 April 1992.

The first of a few more shots from my time on the railway now. This is the excellent view from the Bournemouth signal box, situated high above the station canopy as 47188 passes with just one wagon (again!) that originated at Furzebrook, near Wareham. The whole area in the background was the site of Bournemouth Steam shed until 1967 when steam was abolished. Although still extant, the signal box was closed in 2003. At one time, there was talk that it could be used as some sort of museum but nothing ever came of it. The loco didn't last much longer itself, soldiering on in service until the early 2000s, but it was scrapped during 2005. 19 March 1987.

On the same day as the previous view, this is Railfreight-liveried 47215 passing through the eastern end of Bournemouth station with an empty steel train from Hamworthy Quay. The 4-VEP slam-door unit to the right was waiting to work a stopping service to London Waterloo. This was a very popular spot for photographers prior to 1967 when there was a super semaphore signal gantry here and, of course, steam locos! At this point in time, this loco was allocated to Bristol Bath Road depot but was scrapped (unusually at Eastleigh) during 1993 as a result of accident damage. 19 March 1987.

This time we see the view west from Branksome signal box as 47520 powers through the station with the morning Furzebrook to Fawley oil train. It was quite unusual to see an ETH-fitted Class 47/4 on this service at the time. Branksome signal box was closed in 2003, along with that at Bournemouth. The loco was scrapped during 1998. 17 February 1988.

Right: This is 47249, seemingly dumped in a short siding at Bournemouth TRSMD. None of the class were ever allocated to this depot, so it was unclear why it was here with the buffers removed. It was obviously nothing too serious, however, as the loco carried on in service until it was scrapped in 1998. 17 February 1988.

Below: Not many of the class received Railfreight Construction livery. This, however, is 47210 *Blue Circle Cement* running light at Newport. This had been a life-long Scottish loco until early 1992 when it was transferred to Sheffield Tinsley depot. It was scrapped in 2000. 21 July 1992.

Class 47s: The Jack of All Trades

Looking very smart in its black Waterman Railways livery, this is 47710 *Lady Godiva* at Yeovil Junction. Here to take part in the Yeovil Rail Festival, it was certainly no stranger to this location; however, a couple of years prior to this, it was a regular performer on London Waterloo to Exeter St Davids services. After going on to work with Fragonset Railways, it was scrapped during 2007. 6 October 1994.

We are now at Westbury to see 'Inter-City'-liveried 47841 *The Institution of Mechanical Engineers* passing th rough with the diverted 1V46, the 09.10 Liverpool Lime Street to Plymouth. The more direct section of line normally taken by this train between Bristol and Taunton was closed for engineering work on this day. This loco is now owned by LSL and is currently located at Margate, where it will eventually become a static exhibit in a new museum currently being developed there. 17 February 1996.

This is 47114 passing slowly through Bristol Temple Meads with a china clay train from Cornwall. This was one of five locos originally built as Class 48s, which had a slightly different engine and various other internal differences. They did not last very long, though, as all were converted to standard Class 47s during 1968/69. Later working for Freightliner, this particular loco was scrapped in 2005. 21 July 1992.

BR Days 1985–1999

In an unusual version of 'large logo' livery but with small running numbers, 47814 awaits departure from Exeter St Davids with 1S71, the 08.17 Penzance to Glasgow service, which it worked as far as Birmingham New Street. This loco was completely rebuilt as 57306 during 2003. 5 August 1989.

Now moving to Basingstoke, this is 47376 *Skylark* approaching with a northbound Freightliner service. This loco later became the first of the class to carry the new Freightliner 'triple grey' livery in mid-1995 and was named *Freightliner 1995*. It can now be found preserved in this livery and is fully operational on the Gloucestershire & Warwickshire Railway. 10 July 1992.

The sharp curve at the east end of Salisbury station is the location this time as 47326+47094 pass through with a westbound oil train. On this occasion, 47094 had failed and was rescued en route by 47326. Of these locos, 47094 was scrapped in late 1994, and 47326 met its fate in 2006. 11 April 1990.

Another smart-looking Freightliner loco as Railfreight Distribution-liveried 47351 heads through Southampton Central with an intermodal service heading for Southampton Maritime. This loco was scrapped in early 2001. 10 April 1991.

Coming around the curve on the approach to Hamworthy station, 47287 has charge of a short eastbound freight, which includes a couple of china clay wagons from Furzebrook. A stopping service for Wareham passes in the opposite direction, formed of a 'slam door' unit. This loco had a very uneventful life right up until scrapping, which came in early 2005. 10 April 1990.

The observer at this point today would be hard pushed to realise it is the same location. 47360 is waiting at signals to proceed at Didcot with an eastbound freight that originated in South Wales. As well as the overhead wires that now cover this area, there is also now a huge multi-storey car park that has engulfed the standard car park to the right of the picture. The loco managed to survive until its inevitable scrapping during 2007. 8 December 1992.

Still at Didcot, this is 47738 *Bristol Barton Hill* passing through the station with an unidentified eastbound Royal Scotsman charter. Although this loco was scrapped during 2003, one cab was saved and can now be found in the Health & Safety Interactive Centre opposite Plymouth Station. 11 April 1996.

Up until now in this book, we have seen a few Parcels Sector locos working passenger trains, but this is RES-liveried 47709 doing what it was supposed to! The former ScotRail and Network SouthEast loco is arriving at Reading with a westbound parcels train. After working for some years with Fragonset, the loco was finally scrapped during 2012. 28 September 1995.

This is another unusual 'large logo' livery variation with small numbers under the cab windows. 47822 hauls 43126 through Reading with the up 'Cornish Riviera Express'. The HST power car had failed earlier in the journey and had to be assisted by the 47. This loco may be remembered for when it was numbered 47164 in 1977, as it carried a large Union Flag on its body sides as part of the Queen's Silver Jubilee celebrations. The loco was withdrawn in 2002 but was later rebuilt as 57305 and at the time of writing is rather ironically on long-term hire to GWR! 43126 has since been moved north of the border to operate with ScotRail. 30 August 1989.

Left: To finish this first section, we take a quick look at 47901, which was a power unit test bed loco, firstly for Class 56 (as 47601) and later for Class 58 (47901). It is seen stabled in the early morning autumn sunshine at Reading. The loco was often used on heavy stone trains originating from the Somerset quarries in the late '80s and early '90s, but it was withdrawn during 1990 and scrapped in 1992. 24 October 1987.

Below: An everyday sight during the late 1980s. 47901 stands on Bristol Bath Road depot with a Class 33 for company. Does that engine perched on the low wagon behind the loco come from 47901, I wonder? *Circa* 1987.

Chapter 2

From 2000 to The Present Day

We start our 21st-century section with a few shots of the class operating with Virgin Cross Country. This is 47843 *Vulcan* pulling away from Basingstoke with a southbound service for Poole. This loco is now owned by Rail Operations Group (ROG) but is currently stored unserviceable at Worksop. 17 October 2001.

This is 47848 *Newton Abbot Festival of Transport*, speeding west around the curve past the grounds of Powderham Castle, near Starcross, with 1V42, the 08.05 Liverpool Lime Street to Paignton service. After working with various operators after Virgin Cross Country, the loco is currently operational with WCRC and based at Carnforth. 29 September 2001.

During the late 1990s and early 2000s, Virgin Cross Country found themselves short of locos and as a result often used to hire in RES examples, some of which actually gained Virgin livery. One such is 47722 *The Queen Mother*, seen here passing through Dawlish Warren with 1M25, the 16.17 Paignton to Manchester service. This loco was no stranger to this area, as it had been a Western Region-based example for a large part of its early life. It was scrapped during 2007. 30 June 2001.

This is 47812 passing by Marine Parade at Dawlish with an unidentified service bound for the North. After a similar career to 47848, this loco is now fully operational with WCRC and based at Carnforth. 4 August 2001.

Showing a good amount of 'clag' from the exhaust, 47806 is pulling away from the Teignmouth stop with a service for Paignton. This loco ceased operations with Virgin Cross Country in early 2002 and was rebuilt as 57309 the following year. 30 June 2001.

The next station west of Teignmouth is Newton Abbot, where we see 47711 *County of Hertfordshire* departing with a westbound service. To the right is 47792 *Saint Cuthbert*, which had arrived with a railtour, as this was a day of celebrations in conjunction with the Festival of Transport being held this weekend. That also explains the amount of people milling around! The former ScotRail/Network SouthEast 47711 was withdrawn by Virgin soon after this shot and was scrapped during 2004, whilst 47792 fared much better; later renumbered back to 47804, it is currently in service with WCRC at Carnforth. 13 May 2000.

This is 47826 nearing Starcross with 1V35, the 06.05 Derby to Plymouth service. Unfortunately, this view is now blighted by the addition of railings on top of the sea wall. 9 August 2001.

In the last few months of loco-hauled Virgin Cross Country services, 47826 became something of a 'celebrity' as it was treated to a repaint into 'Inter-City' livery rather than Virgin red. It also received the name *Springburn*, which it had carried when previously numbered 47637. With barely enough light for photography, and very soon after it received this repaint, the loco is seen departing Southampton Central with 1M01, the 06.40 Poole to Liverpool Lime Street service. The loco is currently still in service with WCRC. 24 November 2001.

Left: Waiting to leave the sharply curved platforms at Poole with a northbound service is 47853. This loco has had a very eventful life, but more on that later in this section. 8 September 2001.

Below: As discussed earlier in this book, on Saturdays during the summer months extra trains often ran to/from the popular holiday destination of Weymouth in Dorset. This continued for a while after Virgin took control of Cross Country. 47722 *The Queen Mother* is seen again, this time racing through Wool station with 1M13, the 09.20 Weymouth to Liverpool Lime Street. The signal box to the right has since been demolished. 2 June 2001.

Here we see 47827 approaching Eastleigh with an unidentified northbound service. This loco was withdrawn by Virgin in 2002 but was later rebuilt as 57302. At the time of writing, it is now owned by LSL and is in storage at Eastleigh Works, which is just out of view to the left of this image. 16 April 2000.

With just two months to go until the final Virgin loco-hauled services ran, 47840 *North Star* was one of a few examples to receive a 'heritage' livery by Virgin Cross Country, being repainted back into the once-maligned BR blue livery. The loco is seen arriving at Taunton on one of its first trips out after the repaint with 1M40, the 11.50 Plymouth to Birmingham New Street service. It was also pretty much expected that the loco would eventually be preserved, and that happened in May 2007 when it worked a special Derby to Minehead charter and on into preservation at the West Somerset Railway under its own power. Recently, however, it has gone on long-term loan to the North Yorkshire Moors Railway under the guise of 47077, its first TOPS number. 22 May 2002.

A powerful image of 47830 approaching at speed past the grounds of Powderham Castle with 1A65, the 11.40 Penzance to London Paddington, on the rear of which were two special motor-rail coaches that accommodated private cars. This was an attempt by FGW at reviving days long gone when passengers' motor cars were conveyed by train, but it didn't prove much of a success. More about the loco later in this section. 29 September 2001.

Arriving at the sleepy Somerset station at Castle Cary, this is 47832 *Tamar* with a Plymouth to London Paddington service. As of 2022, this is the loco that has carried the most liveries in its career (of any loco, I think?); the last count, I believe, was 15! More on this one later as well. 22 May 2002.

Left: This is 47816 *Bristol Bath Road – Quality Approved* passing Marine Parade at Dawlish with 1A83, the 16.40 Plymouth to London Paddington service. Despite being withdrawn in 2008, the loco is still languishing at Crewe Depot under Freightliner ownership, very unlikely to work again. 30 July 2002.

Below: 47811 is seen here at Plymouth station with the stock for a London Paddington service. This loco was finally scrapped in November 2022. 14 March 2002.

Teignmouth station is the location this time as we see 47815 *Abertawe Landore* heading east with 1A78, the 15.40 Paignton to London Paddington service. This loco has enjoyed a very different later life than the one seen in the previous picture. After ending its service with FGW, it went on to work with Riviera Trains and then ROG; it is currently in service with WCRC, carrying two-tone green livery and named *Great Western*. 30 June 2001.

Right: Moving to Berkeley Marsh, near Frome, here is 47813 *SS Great Britain* passing with a London Paddington to Plymouth service. This is another loco to have passed through a number of operators since being dispensed with by FGW during the early 2000s. It is currently with WCRC; see also page 72. 27 March 2002.

Below: A lovely bright winter's day at Exeter St Davids sees 47815 *Abertawe Landore* again, this time departing with 1C23, the 10.35 London Paddington to Penzance service. 47811 is attached to the rear. I believe this formation was running on this day *vice* the usual HST set. 1 February 2003.

Like Virgin Cross Country, FGW often found itself short of locos, and this was the case here, with Fragonset 47703 *Hermes* passing through Lostwithiel with a Penzance to London Paddington service. This loco was actually being hired by FGW for an extended period at the time. It is now located at Doncaster Works. 30 August 2002.

A very smart-looking 47237 is seen here approaching Westbury off the Bristol line, hauling some redundant wagons to Eastleigh for storage. Considering it could not provide any ETH, this example has been quite a surprising survivor. Upon withdrawal in the early 2000s, it was put into storage, but was later taken on by DRS, Cotswold Rail and Advenza Freight. At present, it is with WCRC and based at Carnforth but out of service. 9 January 2008.

We now move to some of the last few Class 47/0s to be operated by Freightliner in the mid-2000s. This is 47150, arriving at Westbury with an unusual working, a barrier coach move in conjunction with HST power car moves the previous few days, and had just come up from Plymouth Laira depot. The loco ran round here and continued on to Eastleigh. It was stored in 2008 and finally scrapped during 2010. 6 October 2004.

Another more conventional duty for 47150 at the time was 6M16, the 13.48 Southampton Western Docks to Crewe Gresty Lane car/van train, seen here cautiously approaching Southampton Central station. 29 November 2004.

A tidy-looking 47197 has charge of 6M16 this time as we see it coming out of the docks complex at Millbrook. The loco was withdrawn seven months after the date of this shot and was scrapped during 2008. 7 March 2005.

Captured whilst engaged in shunting duties at Millbrook FLT, this is 47309 *European Rail Operator of The Year*. By this time, many of the remaining 47s were being used for those shunting duties previously done by Class 08 shunters. The 47s did occasionally work more taxing main line services if the need arose, though. This loco was withdrawn during 2007 and then moved to the Wensleydale Railway, but unfortunately it was scrapped in early 2009. 14 April 2004.

Prior to the introduction of more and more Class 66/5s, Freightliner went through a period of minor motive power shortage. Due to this, 47355 *Avocet* was hired in from Fragonset Railways for a short time to assist. The loco is seen here approaching Eastleigh with 4M55, the 08.55 Southampton Maritime to Lawley Street service. It is currently stored at the WCRC base at Carnforth in a dilapidated state and is very unlikely to work again. 27 August 2003.

During 2003, an innovative idea was trialled between Westbury Cement Works and Millbrook FLT using so called 'piggyback' wagons that were operated by Freightliner. This service used dedicated 'drive on, drive off' wagons and road lorries, but, unfortunately, it didn't even last a year. The wagons ended up being exported, whilst Lafarge took over Blue Circle Cement and ended production at Westbury Cement Works. This is 47279, coming off the line from Romsey at Redbridge with 4O77, the 07.37 Westbury Cement Works to Millbrook FLT. The loco was scrapped during 2007. 16 June 2003.

The working seen in the last shot usually worked directly back to Westbury the same way as it arrived, via Redbridge, but on this particular day there was a points problem at the western exit of Millbrook FLT, which meant the train had to go via Eastleigh, then via Chandlers Ford to Romsey and then the booked route to Westbury. I believe this was the only time this happened in the short period it ran. This is 47358 passing Southampton Central with the train. The loco was scrapped in 2009. 31 July 2003.

47358 is seen again, this time approaching Eastleigh in some nice early spring sunshine with a fully loaded southbound liner heading for Southampton Maritime. 19 March 2003.

The last two shots of Freightliner 47s show the popular (at the time) 6M16 car train again. This is 47270 *Cory Brothers 1842-1992* approaching Eastleigh, where there was often a crew change. Thankfully, this loco is now privately owned and back in BR blue livery, named *Swift*, and is currently based at the WCRC headquarters at Carnforth, from where it still sees occasional main line use. 11 April 2003.

Not only Class 47/0s worked 6M16. The bizarre police car-liveried 47829 that formerly worked with Virgin Cross Country was taken on by Freightliner in the mid-2000s and is seen here curving away from the docks complex at Millbrook (Hants). This loco was withdrawn during 2007, but it was not until 2013 that it was finally scrapped. 18 March 2004.

An RES-liveried loco on the 6W53 08.45 Eastleigh Yard to Furzebrook gas tank train was very unusual at the time, probably the result of the rostered loco failing at Eastleigh. 47776 *Respected* is seen at Baiter, on the approach to Poole. The area to the right of the picture has since been built on, with a huge apartment block now dominating the view. This loco is currently stored at Carnforth. *Circa* 2003.

In 2008 47727/739/749 were taken on by Colas Rail and given their striking orange and black livery. This is 47739 *Robin of Templecombe* approaching West Drayton with 6Z47, the 10.05 Dollands Moor to Gloucester New Yard, conveying a long rake of brand-new timber wagons. The view from here now has drastically changed in recent years with the coming of overhead electrification. 31 August 2012.

Another view of 47739 *Robin of Templecombe*, this time at Didcot North Junction, bringing a recently overhauled rail crane south with 6Z81, the 11.30 Washwood Heath to Whitemoor Yard. This loco was later taken on by GBRf, and more recent images of it can be seen later in this section. 23 November 2012.

Of the three locos refurbished for Colas, 47749 *Demelza* and 47727 *Rebecca* were the first two released to traffic, with 47739 following a few months later. The former two are seen here upon release from Eastleigh Works following naming and handover the previous day, working 6Z70, the 10.00 Eastleigh to Eastleigh demonstration run via Basingstoke and Andover. I believe the formation was originally going to Bristol but was changed at the last minute. 47749 is now also at work with GBRf, mainly for hauling units around the system shared with 727/739. It was also reunited with its *City of Truro* nameplates carried for many years; they were first applied in 1965 when this was a Western Region loco. 21 September 2007.

A very gloomy day in Wiltshire sees 47749 *Demelza* producing a fine trail of fumes as it passes Hawkeridge Junction soon after departure with 6Z47, the 11.55 Westbury to Donnington. The driver this day was Robin Gould, after whom 47739 was named; he sadly passed away in 2013. 29 April 2010.

Our last look at Colas 47s finds 47727 *Rebecca* passing Yatton loops with 6Z47, the 10.10 Taunton Fairwater Yard to Cardiff Canton consisting of five wagons, probably for wheel turning on the Canton lathe. This loco is now in service with GBRf, currently wearing Caledonian Blue livery and carrying the name *Edinburgh Castle/Caisteal Dhun Eideann*. 5 April 2013.

For a short time during 2009, Colas Rail operated an interesting service utilising 47s. This is 47848 *Titan Star* + 47805 *Talisman*, powering south through Oxford with 6Z48, the 13.05 Burton West Yard to Dollands Moor empty steel train. Both of these locos are still with us in 2022, 47848 with WCRC, based at Carnforth, and 47805 with LSL, based at Crewe, and are regularly seen on main line charters. 10 September 2009.

A second view of the train on a different date sees 47805 *Talisman* + 47769 *Resolve* up front, arriving at Banbury. 47769 still in Virgin livery was withdrawn in 2013 but is currently in store at Barrow Hill depot, owned by Harry Needle. 22 October 2009.

Immaculate 'large logo' 47580 *County of Essex* is captured here passing through Tilehurst with 6Z47, the 09.04 Tyseley to Ealing Broadway, hauling a track machine. This loco went on to make many main line appearances on various charters from the date of this image, but in 2022 it is now mainly used on the Mid-Norfolk Railway, where it regularly operates. More pictures of this one later in the book. 11 December 2008.

Another immaculate loco. This is 47830 passing through Eastleigh station as 0Z47, the 05.20 Leeds Balm Road to Eastleigh Works. Seen earlier in this section at work for FGW, the loco later resided at Crewe Basford Hall for some years under the ownership of Freightliner, where it deteriorated. However, in 2015, it was refurbished and repainted and is seen here whilst it was on hire to ROG for a short while. 18 September 2015.

BEECHING'S LEGACY

Oh dear! The intervening seven years since the previous image was taken has not been kind to that gleaming paintwork. Now used by Freightliner as a route learning/driver training loco, it was moved from Crewe Basford Hall to Southampton Maritime in early 2022. Now named *Beeching's Legacy*, the loco is seen here at Gillingham, Dorset, whilst working 0Z47, the 08.30 Southampton Maritime to Southampton Maritime via Redbridge, Salisbury and Exeter St Davids. Locos of any description are rare at this location nowadays. 21 July 2022.

47714 was the first 47/7 to be transferred south after use by ScotRail during 1989 and worked for Network SouthEast until the mid-1990s. After this, it was used by Anglia in the mid-2000s, mainly as a 'Thunderbird' loco for Great Eastern Main Line services. It then went on to work with Cotswold Rail for a while, but in recent years it can be found stored at Doncaster Wabtec awaiting future developments. 15 November 2006.

It is a shame that WCRC did not stick to this livery for its locos. 47854 is seen at Salisbury whilst running around 'Green Express Railtours' 1Z47, the 05.30 Leeds to Salisbury. This was during the early days of WCRC, which were toying with liveries to settle on, and only a couple of locos appeared like this. It is still in service with WCRC to this day. 3 May 2004.

Also at Salisbury, this is 47853 *Rail Express*, which on this day was involved with 1Z37, the 05.23 Derby to Salisbury 'The Salisbury Spire' charter run by Kingfisher Railtours, and also featuring steam loco 34067 *Tangmere*. Originally numbered D1733, this loco was chosen for the XP64 project to find a new corporate BR image in the mid-1960s. As part of this experiment, it was painted at Derby Works in a shade of light blue in April 1964. The proposed new logo for BR, the now famous double-arrow motif, was displayed on all four cabs with a red-painted background. At the time, the logo had not actually been sanctioned by the BR board, and was later removed. The official launch, however, took place in May 1964, but the livery was actually rejected, and when the new image was eventually agreed upon, the shade of blue chosen was quite a bit darker. The new double-arrow logo was still applied to each cab, but the red-painted background was dropped. Many years later, under the ownership of Virgin Trains, a small batch of 'heritage' repaints in 2001 saw the loco regain the XP64 livery, complete with the red-and-white cabside logos. Of course, the final version of BR Rail Blue livery was later applied en masse to many diesel locos, including this one. 1 October 2005.

From 2000 to The Present Day

Now for a few images of charter trains worked by the class. A couple of years after the previous shot, we see 47853 *Rail Express* again, this time at Weymouth, waiting to depart with 1Z46, the 17.12 Weymouth to Norwich 'South Coast Explorer', organised by NENTA Train Tours. In 2022, this loco is now operating with LSL, in standard BR blue and carrying its earlier number 47614. 11 August 2007.

Another of the aforementioned 'heritage' repaints carried out by Virgin in the early 2000s was two-tone green 47851 *Traction Magazine*, just departing the delightful City of Bath on St George's Day with an ECS charter from Leeds, which was heading to Westbury to lay over until its return to Bath later in the day. 23 April 2009.

Unfortunately operating for just one year, the famous Blue Pullman train of the 1960/70s was recreated by Fragonset during 2006. This involved the painting of a rake of stock and two locos in the Nanking Blue livery carried by the original sets. The locos involved were 47709+47712. Here we see 47712 *Artemis* on the rear of this smart-looking train as it enters the depot area at Salisbury on St Valentine's Day. The train had worked in on 1Z40, the 09.20 Stevenage to Salisbury. A number of years later, LSL have also now recreated this train, but this time utilising an HST set. 14 February 2006.

An interesting combination of 47773+33025 is seen here passing Aller Junction, just west of Newton Abbot, with 1Z26, the 17.45 Kingswear to Tyseley Warwick Road 'Dartmouth Royal Regatta' charter. The Class 47 is maintained by Vintage Trains at Tyseley whilst the Class 33 is still in service with WCRC. 30 August 2008.

This time we see the immaculate 47773 again, this time passing Dawlish Warren on the rear of 1Z70, the 06.59 Dorridge to Plymouth charter hauled by preserved 50050 *Fearless*. 24 August 2022.

DRS is another operator of charter trains, and one of its first efforts was the short-lived 'Stobart Pullman' in the mid-2000s. This is the actual launch train, with 47712 *Pride of Carlisle*, arriving at Southampton Central with 1Z88, the 10.43 London Victoria to Fareham (then on to London Euston). 12 February 2008.

The following month, we see the 'Stobart Pullman' once again, but this time at the southern exit of Bincombe Tunnel as 47802 *Pride of Cumbria* nears its destination with 1Z86, the 06.35 Northampton to Weymouth 'Thomas Hardy Circular Tour'. This loco is now in regular service with WCRC. 1 March 2008.

Another view of the train seen in the previous image as the smart-looking loco rests 'on the blocks' at Weymouth station. The DRS 'compass' livery was certainly very striking. 1 March 2008.

DRS also used to provide locos for the luxurious 'Northern Belle' Pullman train for a time in the 2000s. This is 47810 *Peter Bath MBE 1927-2006*, passing through the London suburbs at Lewisham with the 1Z50 Norwich to Hither Green working. 19 May 2011.

Right: Another 'Northern Belle' charter as 47818 passes Bapton (between Salisbury & Warminster) with the 1Z72 Eastleigh to Cardiff Central. This loco is still fully operational, but has only been used for shunting in the depot complex at Eastleigh for quite a few years now. 25 June 2011.

Below: Rounding the curve at Crofton on the Berks & Hants line, this is another 'Northern Belle' charter, with Pullman-liveried 47790 *Galloway Princess* hauling 1Z45, the 05.54 Derby to Newbury 'Historic Bath/Highclere Castle'. This loco is now owned by LSL, restored to 'large logo' livery and with its former number, 47593. 30 August 2012.

During the mid-2010s, DRS also operated a few special boat train services to/from Southampton Docks, reviving memories of days past when the Southern Railway regularly used to run them. In the weak winter sunshine, this is 47853 *Rail Express* passing Worting Junction, just west of Basingstoke with 5Z91, the 12.45 Eastleigh to Crewe Gresty Bridge ECS. The last of these trains ran just over a week later. 4 December 2012.

One of the more recent main line operators has been the aforementioned LSL, which is rapidly becoming established with the running of various charter trains throughout the UK. This is 47614+47593 *Galloway Princess* passing Fairwood Junction, just west of Westbury, with 1Z72, the 06.20 Wolverhampton to Paignton 'Statesman' charter. Strangely enough, although the leading loco carries the numbers 47614, it still shows on the TOPS system as 47853. 30 June 2021.

The next month, 47614 is seen paired with 47828 after arrival at Weymouth with 1Z45, the 06.00 Chester to Weymouth 'Dorset Coast Statesman'. 31 July 2021.

On the same day as the previous shot was taken, this is 47828+47614 at Radipole, commencing the long climb out of Weymouth with 1Z47, the 16.37 Weymouth to Chester return railtour. Hard to believe now, but this was once the location of Radipole Halt station up until its closure in the mid-1980s. 47828 is actually owned by D05 Preservation Ltd and is on short-term hire to LSL for main line work. 31 July 2021.

Right: With the A303 road bridge in the background, this time we see 47593 *Galloway Princess* + 47805 *Roger Hosking MA 1925-2013* passing Wylye foot crossing, between Warminster and Salisbury, with 1Z30, the 06.15 Crewe to Weymouth 'Dorset Coast Statesman' charter. 16 September 2020.

Below: This location is Sheepcote Curve, just north of Bruton in Somerset, as 47810 *Crewe Diesel Depot* + 47805 *Roger Hosking MA 1925-2013* pass by in the evening sunshine on St George's Day with 1Z80, the 16.37 Paignton to Ely 'English Riviera Statesman' charter. 23 April 2022.

Above: 47614+47805 *Roger Hosking MA 1925-2013* are captured here at Culliford Road bridge on the approach to Dorchester South with 1Z80, the 06.09 Norwich to Weymouth charter. It is also hard to believe that this was a double-track main line up until the Moreton to Dorchester section was singled in 1985. 9 July 2022.

Left: From a vantage point high above Bincombe Tunnel, 47805 now leads 47614 with the return 1Z82, the 16.36 Weymouth to Norwich charter, which was delayed due to an earlier track circuit failure. Part of the seaside town of Weymouth can be seen in the background, with the English Channel beyond. 9 July 2022.

We are now at Wimbledon West Junction to see spotless 47805 *Roger Hosking MA 1925-2013* approaching with 1Z22, the 09.45 London Victoria to Alresford private charter operated by Saphos Trains. 31 August 2018.

47810 (originally D1924) has a big story to tell, especially if you were a Southern Railway enthusiast back at the very end of steam operations in 1967. Many of these steam fans were convinced that the final runs of the famous London Waterloo to Bournemouth 'Bournemouth Belle' Pullman and return workings were going to be steam-hauled on the final day of steam working on the Southern on 9 July 1967. Instead, both services were hauled by, you guessed it, D1924! It is therefore incredible that the same loco, in almost the same livery (though looking far better than it did back then!) and even on the same down fast line at Farnborough along which it hauled that famous train 55 years ago, is racing through with 1Z31, the 05.04 Doncaster to Portsmouth Harbour 'Statesman' charter. The only obvious difference this time around is the *Crewe Diesel Depot* nameplate.   23 March 2022.

A nice bit of 'clag' from the exhaust now as 47593 *Galloway Princess* pulls away from Salisbury with 1Z60, the 06.35 Poole to Kingswear 'English Riviera Express' charter. 2 July 2022.

Class 47s: The Jack of All Trades

47593 *Galloway Princess* is seen again, this time powering west at Powderham, near Starcross, with 1Z86, the 05.12 Nottingham to Kingswear 'Dartmouth Regatta Statesman'. Since the provision of a footbridge at this location to replace a dangerous foot crossing, it has proved to be a great photographic vantage point. 31 August 2019.

Immaculate BR green pair 47501 *Craftsman* + 47810 *Crewe Diesel Depot* are passing Taunton with 1Z47, the 05.10 Crewe to Paignton 'English Riviera Statesman' charter. Since this image was taken, 47501 has been stored, though probably only temporarily. 27 July 2019.

Another example to have worked on the main line in the popular 'large logo' livery (with the addition of a large Union Flag) is 47580 *County of Essex*. The first of a few shots sees it passing Mount Pleasant level crossing, near Southampton, with the 5Z90 Southall to Weymouth ECS for a steam charter running the following day. This loco can currently be found on the Mid-Norfolk Railway. 22 November 2013.

From 2000 to The Present Day

Soon after arrival at its destination with the 1Z82 from Ashford, this is 47580 *County of Essex* at Salisbury station. It was later detached from the train and ran round, ready to work the return later in the day after a layover in the sidings. 12 December 2015.

Right: There is surely no mistaking this location as 47580 *County of Essex* passes Marine Parade at Dawlish with 1Z62, the 06.30 Alresford (Hants) to Paignton 'Cathedrals Express' charter. 16 August 2018.

Below: Here we see 47580 *County of Essex* + 47760 passing over Wallington Viaduct on the approach to Fareham with 1Z61, the 07.51 West Brompton to Bristol Temple Meads 'Cathedrals Express' charter. This was originally advertised as a steam-hauled train, but the unavailability of both first and second choice of locos meant it was eventually hauled throughout by these two 47s. 13 April 2016.

Class 47s: The Jack of All Trades

Taken from the footbridge that has since been consigned to history, this is **47727** *Edinburgh Castle / Caisteal Dhun Eideann*, approaching Millbrook (Hants) with 1Z53, the 07.17 Cardiff Central to Portsmouth Harbour 'Solent & Sussex Explorer'. To date, a GBRf Class 47 has only featured on a handful of charters. 66741 *Swanage Railway* is on the rear. 21 July 2018.

A very unusual combination now as 47712 *Artemis* + 71000 *Duke of Gloucester* are captured approaching Dorchester South almost two hours late, with 1Z91, the 08.36 Kensington Olympia to Weymouth 'Sunny South Special'. The unique steam loco unfortunately failed earlier in the journey at Totton, just west of Southampton, the Class 47 being taken off the rear of the train and led through to Weymouth. This shot was taken from Dorchester South signal box. 3 August 2005.

Displaying one of its record number of liveries, this is 47832, just arrived at Oxford with 1Z47, the 09.55 Stevenage to Oxford private charter. Personally, I thought this one-off Victa Westlink Rail livery looked quite smart, but it was very short lived, with this loco being the sole vehicle ever to wear it. 22 November 2007.

Eleven years later (and a few more liveries!), this is 47832 in its current guise, soon after departing Westbury with the 1Z65 Swindon to Weymouth 'Northern Belle' charter.
15 July 2018.

As can be judged by earlier images, the luxurious 'Northern Belle' Pullman train is a major source of employment for WCRC locos. This time, 47826 is seen passing the famous location of Langstone Rock on the South Devon sea wall near Dawlish Warren with 1Z57, the 11.30 Bristol Temple Meads to Par.
8 July 2022.

The train often has a quite intensive itinerary over the summer months. Just the following day, 47826 is seen again, emerging from what looks like a jungle on the approach to Dorchester South with 1Z47, the 08.23 Birmingham International to Weymouth. 9 July 2022.

On the same day as the previous shot, an immaculate 47813 is passing Dorchester West station with 1Z28, the 13.59 Yeovil Junction to Weymouth section of the 'End of Southern Steam' charter that mainly featured SR Pacific 35028 *Clan Line*. There was a track circuit failure in this area at the time, causing much delay and operating headaches. 9 July 2022.

Exactly 12 years earlier and a few miles further north than the previous image, this is 47760 on the single line just south of Yetminster with an almost identical 1Z97, the 14.00 Yeovil Junction to Weymouth 'Dorset Coast Express'. The main feature of this charter this time was Royal Scot loco 46115 *Scots Guardsman*. The 47 is still with WCRC but is currently out of service at Carnforth. 9 July 2010.

During the summer months, WCRC also make use of their non Class 47/0s that have not been fitted with train heating. 47245 draws into the sidings at Poole with the ECS 'Bath & Bristol Steam Express' hauled by 'Britannia' Pacific 70013 *Oliver Cromwell*, which was attached to the other end of the train at this point. This particular Class 47 is very much at home on the former Southern Region. As D1922, when it was just a few years old it was one of just four or five of the class that were allocated to Eastleigh depot from late 1966 until early 1968 to help out at the very end of Southern steam services, covering for any shortages that might occur. The loco is still in service with WCRC. 30 May 2009.

Mentioned earlier, the other Class 47/0 to see regular service over the years with WCRC has been 47237. It is seen here at Hawkeridge Junction, on the approach to Westbury with 5Z68, the 09.56 Bath Spa to Westbury 'Royal Scotsman' empty stock move. 9 July 2013.

This is 47805 *Talisman* soon after arriving at its destination with 1Z45, the 04.50 Norwich to Weymouth 'South Coast Explorer' operated by NENTA Railtours. The loco is in the blue livery of Riviera Trains and carried it for a few years before being taken on by DRS. However, it is now back in two-tone green and operating with LSL. 11 August 2007.

Some years earlier, we see another NENTA Railtours charter. This is the 'South Coast Explorer', passing Poole with 47793 *Saint Augustine* on its return from Weymouth to Norwich. This loco has since been preserved and can currently be found on the Mid-Hants Railway in its former guise as 47579 *James Nightall GC*. 7 July 2001.

Another loco to be used by Riviera Trains is 47812, seen here at Norton Bavant, just east of Warminster, with 5Z47, the 13.35 Bristol to Eastleigh empty stock move. This was the rake of stock used for the 'Torbay Express' steam-hauled charters during the summer, being tripped back after the season had finished. After a stint with ROG, the loco is now with WCRC at Carnforth. 25 September 2012.

Only a handful of the fleet ever gained the EWS red and gold livery. One such was 47778 *Duke of Edinburgh's Award*, captured heading west at Wyke Champflower, near Castle Cary, with an unidentified charter. Despite the loco looking very smart, it was scrapped just three years later, in 2006. 1 March 2003.

This is the first of a mix of various workings by the class. During the time of a shortage of DMUs, when locos were being used in top-and-tail mode on the so-called 'short set' for Greater Anglia Trains, this is 47810 *Peter Bath MBE 1927-2006* top-and-tailing 47818 approaching their destination with the 14.36 Norwich to Yarmouth. The consist of the short train also includes DVT 82136. 21 February 2014.

The famous pop festival held at Glastonbury attracts many thousands of people every year it is held, with a great deal of these arriving by train at the nearest station, Castle Cary. Back in the days when extra stock and locos could be mustered up without too much difficulty, this is 47749 *Atlantic College* top-and-tailing 47789 *Lindisfarne* on the approaches to Westbury with one of the few Castle Cary to Westbury and return shuttles that ran this day to cater for the crowds. After a few operators, 47749 is still giving sterling service for GBRf, hauling various units around the UK. 47789, however, was scrapped in 2007. 28 June 2002.

Looking very much like a Virgin Cross Country service that had ceased running the previous year, this is 47488, waiting to depart from a very dull Weymouth station with a rake of Mk2 coaches that had been used as barriers for the commissioning of South West Trains' new 'Desiro' EMUs. This loco often worked on the main line, supporting steam specials etc. during the early 2000s, but the working seen here turned out to be one of its last, if not the last. Surprisingly, though, it was not scrapped and has now been in storage for almost 20 years, currently rusting away quietly at Nemesis Rail at Burton-on-Trent. 20 November 2003.

This is quite possibly the last time a member of the class worked an inspection saloon special, I believe due to none of the regular Class 37s being available. By this date, 47s were very rarely seen escorting 975025 *Caroline*, but this is 47818, propelling the saloon at Millbrook (Hants) on the 2Z02 West Brompton to West Brompton, which ran via Woking, Andover, Redbridge, Southampton, Portsmouth, Guildford, Wokingham, Reading, Basingstoke and Woking back to West Brompton. This loco still sees occasional use within the confines of Eastleigh Works, as a shunting loco. 19 August 2015.

The famous red cliffs dominate the view as we see 47815 *Lost Boys 68-88* + 47812 passing beneath Rockstone Footbridge, Dawlish with 5L46, the 09.00 Plymouth Laira TRSMD to Ely Papworth Sidings, hauling redundant HST stock for further storage. Both of these locos are now working with WCRC, with 47815 now having regained two-tone green livery and reuniting with its former *Great Western* nameplates. 17 December 2018.

Just four months after the previous shot was taken, 47813 is now in ROG livery and carrying the name *Jack Frost* as it is again seen in harness with 47815 *Lost Boys 68-88*, passing Sprey Point at Teignmouth with 5L46, the 08.35 Plymouth Laira TRSMD to Ely Papworth Sidings, hauling yet more redundant HST stock for storage. 11 April 2019.

ROG is also involved with the moving of various EMUs around the system, and here we see 47813 *Jack Frost* once again, this time approaching Eastleigh hauling 'Wessex Electric' unit 2422 as 5Q87, the 09.40 Bournemouth T&RSMD to Eastleigh Works via a loco run-round at Poole. The unit was going for internal refurbishment at the time, but the following year the whole Class 442 fleet was suddenly consigned to the scrapheap after a shock change of plan by South Western Railway. 17 September 2019.

A redundant HST stock move, undertaken by GBRf 47727 *Edinburgh Castle / Caisteal Dhun Eideann* + 47749 *City of Truro*. They are captured passing through Parson Street, just west of Bristol Temple Meads with 5Z43, the 08.56 Plymouth Laira TRSMD to Long Marston, with coaches for further storage. 3 June 2019.

Some years prior to its transfer to Colas Rail and then to GBRf, EWS-liveried 47727 *Castell Caerffili / Caerphilly Castle* is seen approaching Didcot Parkway, hauling two parcel vans as 5A24, the 07.45 Bristol Barton Hill to Old Oak Common. The whole area around here is now somewhat different these days, with the clutter of overhead wires and masts marring the view. 26 February 2003.

Another of the EWS-liveried locos, 47744 is seen here arriving at Exeter St Davids hauling ex-London North Eastern Railway (LNER) A3 Pacific 4472 *Flying Scotsman* and its support coach. The steam loco had worked a London Victoria to Newton Abbot charter earlier in the day as part of the Newton Abbot 2000 festival. The 47 was withdrawn from service in 2003 but is still in storage nearly 20 years later at Nemesis Rail, Burton-on-Trent. 13 May 2000.

This is another unusual move involving a steam loco as we see 47500 passing through Eastleigh hauling 'Merchant Navy' Pacific 35005 *Canadian Pacific*, which had come from the Mid-Hants Railway and was heading to the nearby Eastleigh Works, where it was actually built back in 1941. The steam loco had been a regular main line performer for many years prior to this and was going to the works for a heavy overhaul. The once 'celebrity' 47 (see page 7) was not so lucky, however. During early 2013, it suffered a serious fire, causing it to be withdrawn from service and, after various spares were used for other members of the class, the loco was finally scrapped during 2020 at Carnforth. 22 September 2011.

Far better off was 47810, which is seen here being towed by 66140 through Eastleigh in primer after a heavy overhaul in Eastleigh Works. The loco was later taken in the consist of 4Z47 (Eastleigh to Crewe) for painting into two-tone green for LSL. See also page 67. 18 April 2018.

Absolutely immaculate 47727 *Edinburgh Castle / Caisteal Dhun Eideann* is seen here at Basingstoke waiting for the signal to head south. It is towing 73970 as 0Z73, the 09.00 Leicester LIP to Eastleigh Arlington, for bogie attention to the Class 73. Since conversion to 73/9s, the 'Caledonian Sleeper' Class 73s are very rare in the south. 12 September 2019.

Right: The latest incarnation for 47739, as we see the loco at Crediton now sporting a pleasing deep blue livery of GBRf. It is working 0Z47, the 10.10 Exeter St Davids to Coleford, as a GBRf route learner for forthcoming planned engineering work. Notice the extra sockets (also on 47727 in the previous shot) within the headcode panel, which are used in conjunction with unit haulage. 8 October 2019.

Below: Another view of the loco in the bay platform at Exeter St Davids later the same day. 8 October 2019.

Some brief views of the class on test trains now, to finish this section. Firstly, we see 47727 *Duke of Edinburgh's Award* again, this time in its earlier RES livery and passing Poole with an unidentified northbound test train. 9 September 2001.

Another unidentified test train is seen here at Weymouth with 47746 *The Bobby* up front. This loco is currently operational with WCRC and now carries the name *Chris Fudge 29.7.70-22.6.10*. 16 January 2003.

From 2000 to The Present Day

Bathed in the winter sunshine, this is 47776 *Respected*, coming up towards Worgret Junction on what is now part of the Swanage Railway with a test train. When it was still BR-owned, this section of line was freight-only for a few miles as far as Furzebrook and was sporadically visited by test trains to check all was well. The loco is currently stored at the WCRC headquarters at Carnforth, but is unlikely to ever work again. 15 January 2001.

Very unusually, this is 47757 *Capability Brown*, seen shunting its test train around in Jubilee Sidings at Weymouth. The reason for this manoeuvring was due to the loco running solo on this occasion and not in the conventional top-and-tail mode with two locos, thus requiring a good deal more shunting around. The loco was scrapped during 2006. 14 November 2003.

Chapter 3

Open Days and Heritage Lines

When the various depots around the country used to open their doors for annual open days, it was not just the good and the great locos on show. This is recently withdrawn 47001 at Crewe, being 'cabbed' by youngsters. Everything was far more relaxed in those days, and I doubt this sort of thing would be allowed now. Despite its number, this loco was not the first built, but it was the first 'standard' loco after the first batch of 20 (D1500–D1520) that had various mechanical differences. A preservation offer fell through and the loco was finally scrapped in 1993. 4 July 1987.

This is a view that is now impossible to repeat. A spotless 'Inter-City'-liveried 47805 is positioned on the turntable at Bristol Bath Road depot during an open day, with covered nameplates. At a ceremony later in the day, these were revealed as *Bristol Bath Road*. This loco, however, carried these plates for only a few years until they were transferred to 47816. Over 30 years later, 47805 is still at work on the national network, back in two-tone green livery with LSL. Unfortunately, Bristol Bath Road depot is no longer extant; it was closed in September 1995 and the whole site cleared for redevelopment, which at the time of writing three decades on, is still yet to commence. 29 June 1991.

An interesting event took place at Exeter Riverside yard in May 1994. The occasion was to celebrate the connection the City of Exeter has had with railways for 150 years from 1844 to 1994. It proved to be a very popular event. Inevitably Class 47s were represented and this is D1524 (47004) *Old Oak Common Traction & Rolling Stock Depot*, showing off its recently applied 'heritage' livery to good effect. Continuing in main line service until the early 2000s, it was later bought for preservation by a private individual and can now be found on the Embsay & Bolton Abbey Railway, albeit currently stored out of service. 5 May 1994.

Another example on show at the Exeter Railfair was 47085 *REPTA 1893-1993* in an equally resplendent Railfreight Distribution livery. The loco was quite at home here; when new, it was D1670 *Mammoth* and was allocated to the Western Region. Despite the obvious immaculate appearance, the loco it was scrapped in the late 1990s. 5 May 1994.

Another Crewe open day, and more shabby locos! 47539 (the former *Rochdale Pioneers*) is seen awaiting its fate. Although the date of this image is 2000, it was not actually withdrawn until the following year, with scrapping following during 2002. 20 May 2000.

Displaying the obvious fire damage which led to its demise, this is 47971 (formerly *Robin Hood*), looking very sorry for itself at the same Crewe open day as the previous shot. Interestingly, apart from its original number (D1616), this loco also carried the numbers 47480/97480. It was officially withdrawn two months after the date of this picture and was scrapped during 2002. 20 May 2000.

Still at Crewe but a few years after the previous image, this is 47798 *Prince William* on display in its full Royal regalia. This loco (and 47799 *Prince Henry*) had been given this livery during 1995, the pair comprising the dedicated Royal Train locos until their withdrawal in 2004 when new 67005 and 67006 were repainted to replace them. This loco eventually became part of the National Collection at York but the current status of 47799, latterly preserved on the Eden Valley Railway, is uncertain. 31 May 2003.

One of the most well-known rail events of the 1980s was the Basingstoke Railfair. It was held in late September 1987 and, like the event at Exeter, was also very well attended. This is 47581 *Great Eastern* in the early version of Network SouthEast livery. At this time based at Stratford, it eventually found its way to Old Oak Common for Oxford/Newbury services out of London Paddington. Upon cessation of these loco-hauled passenger services with Network SouthEast, the loco operated for a number of years with RES under the number 47763. It was finally scrapped during 2003. 26 September 1987.

This is 47306 *The Sapper* on display at Old Oak Common open day. Most of the 47/3 sub-class led quite ordinary lives, with many escaping the preservationists. As they were not fitted with train heating, their use was restricted to freight trains and occasional passenger use during the summer months. This loco can now be found fully operational on the Bodmin & Wenford Railway in Cornwall.
5 August 2000.

On the same day as the previous shot, this is First Great Western's 47846 *Thor*, looking very smart. At the time, this loco was still in frontline service with FGW. It was, however, withdrawn a couple of years after this shot, only to emerge totally rebuilt in early 2003 as 57308, which is still in service in 2022 with DRS.
5 August 2000.

Inside one of the depot buildings at Old Oak Common, this is D1924 (47004) *Old Oak Common Traction & Rolling Stock Depot* that we saw earlier at Exeter. As you can imagine, it became the depot favourite for a few years.
5 August 2000.

D1524 (47004) *Old Oak Common Traction & Rolling Stock Depot* was also a popular choice for attending diesel galas at various heritage lines throughout the UK. It is seen here between duties at Bewdley on the Severn Valley Railway. 29 September 2000.

Here we see 47105, soon after arrival at Toddington on the Gloucestershire & Warwickshire Railway. This was one of the earliest locos to be preserved, entering private ownership in early 1994. 27 December 2000.

This is the daddy of the class! 47401 *North Eastern* is seen here beside the loco depot at Swanwick Junction at the Midland Railway Centre. Built and entering service in late 1962, the loco has just turned 60 years old with hopefully plenty of years' service still ahead of it. As the first 20 locos built were all mechanically non-standard to the rest of the class, they were early withdrawal candidates from BR service. That came for this loco in June 1992, but in 1994 it was rescued for preservation. 23 June 2001.

This is 47596, running round its train at Wymondham on the Mid-Norfolk Railway. This is believed to be one of its first runs in preservation back in BR blue livery. The loco was withdrawn in late 2002 and was saved for preservation during 2006. 16 March 2007.

Another view of 47596, this time at Dereham as it pulls away with a train for Wymondham. Since this date, the loco has carried a few more liveries, including the revised Network SouthEast colours and the *Aldeburgh Festival* name that it is perhaps best remembered for carrying between 1989 and 1993. 16 March 2007.

North of the border, this is 47643, seen waiting to depart Bo'ness station on the Bo'ness & Kinneil Railway. This loco has always been based in Scotland from new and is preserved in the ScotRail (red stripe) livery that it was withdrawn in back in 1992. In fact, since it was renumbered 47643 in early 1986, it has worn no other livery, as far as I am aware. Unusually, especially for a passenger loco, it has never carried a name. 2 September 2000.

Left: Back south now as we reach the Mid-Hants Railway. A few examples have worked on this line, often during the diesel galas held there during the early 2000s. This is 47224 *Arcidae*, stabled at a rather wet Alresford between duties at the 2003 Diesel Gala. At this time, the loco was still in main line service with Freightliner, but was scrapped in 2007. 16 May 2003.

Below: On the same day as the previous shot, this is 47224 *Arcidae*, pulling away from Alresford with a train for Alton. 16 May 2003.

Seen earlier at the Old Oak Common open day, this is 47306 *The Sapper* + 33208 arriving at Medstead & Four Marks station with an Alresford to Alton service during the 2002 diesel gala. Around this time there was a rather silly craze for loco headboards, which is taken to the extreme here, somewhat ruining the image in my opinion. 26 April 2002.

IVANHOE

More crazy headboards as 47358 *Ivanhoe* + 33208 get away from Ropley with an Alresford to Alton service, whilst to the left is a failed 47303 *Freightliner Cleveland*. The name on 47358, which was one of the very last in service with Freightliner at this time, was painted on and unofficial. It was scrapped during 2007. More on 47303 next. 14 May 2005.

47303 *Freightliner Cleveland* was unfortunately declared a failure on this day, as it had flat batteries. It can be seen here connected up to a charger, but despite this, I don't think it played any further part in the gala. The loco was also one of the last in service with Freightliner, being withdrawn around the same time as 47358 and scrapped in 2007. 14 May 2005.

Visiting from the East Lancs Railway, its base at the time, this is second-built D1501 (47402) (formerly *Gateshead*), seen here climbing the bank between Ropley and Medstead & Four Marks with an Alresford to Alton service during the 2013 diesel gala. Withdrawn around the same time as 47401 *North Eastern* mentioned earlier, the loco was saved for preservation in late 1993. More recently the loco has moved to Peak Rail, Derbyshire. 26 April 2013.

Moving further west, we now see a couple of the class on the East Somerset Railway. During the early 2000s, the line held a couple of interesting diesel galas. Although the line is quite short, there are a few good vantage points. This is 47758, producing a marvellous display of 'clag' as it comes through the rock cutting about midway along the line with a train for Mendip Vale. The loco was scrapped during 2008. 6 April 2003.

Mendip Vale is a rudimentary one-platform station that was constructed to form the temporary terminus of the line and to enable a loco to run round its train; there was never a station here originally. The small station can just be made out in the exhaust haze here as 47758 heads back towards Cranmore. The original plan was to try and extend the line to Shepton Mallet, which is only about a mile or so distant, but problems arose when looking for a site for some sort of station and those ambitions are currently curtailed, it seems. Many years ago, a station actually existed at Shepton Mallet (High Street) but, unfortunately, that was erased from the map upon closure of the line and is today, perhaps inevitably, a supermarket. 6 April 2003.

CRANMORE FOUR

Above: Another view of 47365 outside the depot at Cranmore. Note that it has gained a painted name, *Cranmore Four*! Externally, at least, the loco didn't look too bad. 17 April 2004.

Right: Many of the class were still being withdrawn from BR service during the early 2000s, one such being 47365 (formerly *Diamond Jubilee*), which is seen here in a sorry state outside the loco shed at Cranmore. The intention was to restore the loco to service using the facilities here, but unfortunately this plan never got off the ground and the loco was scrapped in 2007. 17 April 2004.

Moving south again now and we reach the Swanage Railway, which has seen a fair share of the class to date, mostly during diesel galas. This is 1842 (47192), crossing Corfe Common with a Norden to Swanage train during the 2017 diesel gala. This loco was withdrawn from BR service during 1988 but became the first of the class to be preserved as long ago as 1990, meaning it has now been in preservation about as long as it was in BR service. 5 May 2017.

1842 (47192) is seen again, this time approaching Quarr Farm level crossing with a Swanage-bound train. The 5A shed plate on the front of the loco refers to Crewe North, the first depot it was allocated to from new in 1965. The loco has since received a full two-tone green repaint with small yellow warning panels. 5 May 2017.

Another popular visitor for the 2014 diesel gala was 'large logo' 47292, seen here departing Corfe Castle with a Swanage to Norden train. This loco managed to last in service with Freightliner until the end of 2003 and was saved for preservation in 2007. Its current home is the Churnet Valley Railway. 9 May 2014.

At the time of this image of 'large logo' 47635 crossing Corfe Viaduct, it was resident at Swanage, where it stayed for just over a year during 2007/08. Withdrawn by BR in 2004, the loco had briefly carried the name *The Lass O`Ballochmyle*, but, as can be seen by the scar on the bodyside, this was removed upon the loco's withdrawal from service. Previously to this, it had been named *Jimmy Milne* back in 1987 and it is that name that it once again carries today at its base on the Epping Ongar Railway. 12 April 2008.

An almost head-on view of 47635 this time as it comes beneath the main A351 road bridge at Afflington, between Corfe Castle and Harmans Cross, with a Swanage-bound train. It is interesting to see the distinct gradient change here through a telephoto lens. 12 April 2008.

Next we head to the West Somerset Railway, where we see an immaculate D1661 (47840) *North Star* that had recently been restored to near-original condition at its birthplace of Brush Works, Loughborough. On completion of the overhaul, it worked a 1Z47 Derby to Minehead train under its own power and into preservation. More recently, the loco has been returned to BR blue livery, carrying its earlier identity of 47077, and is currently on long-term loan to the North Yorkshire Moors Railway. 16 June 2007.

In some lovely afternoon sunshine, D1661 *North Star* is seen this time at Bishops Lydeard, having arrived with a train from Minehead. 17 June 2007.

Above: A final view of D1661 *North Star* as it rounds the curve on the approach to Doniford Halt with a Minehead to Bishops Lydeard train. 12 June 2009.

Left: To end this Class 47s volume, we have a few shots taken on the South Devon Railway. Still in service with Freightliner at the time, 47197 is seen on a demonstration goods train near Staverton during the 2004 diesel gala. This loco was scrapped in early 2008. 18 June 2004.

Another view of 47197, this time surrounded by semaphore signals in the loop at Staverton. 18 June 2004.

During the 2003 gala, we see Freightliner-liveried 47279, piloting resident loco 25262 and waiting to proceed towards Staverton with a train for Totnes Littlehempston. 47279 saw service with Freightliner until withdrawal in early 2004 and was scrapped in 2007. 11 May 2003.

Those hideous headboards raise their heads again! 47375 is seen piloting resident loco D6737 (37037) away from Totnes Littlehempston with a train for Buckfastleigh. This example is one of the 47/3s with a somewhat more interesting life history, at least in later years. In 2007, it was taken on by the long-defunct Advenza Freight (whose livery it is wearing here) for a couple of years until it was withdrawn in early 2009. After this, it was moved to Booth's scrapyard. However, it was then moved for further storage at the Dartmoor Railway until 2015, when it was acquired by Continental Railway Solution and after restoration work it was exported to Hungary, of all places. 26 April 2008.

To conclude, we see 47375+31108 passing the delightful River Dart at Hood Bridge with a Totnes Littlehempston to Buckfastleigh service. It is a shame that the river was not slightly calmer; the reflection would then have been perfect! 26 April 2008.

Other books you might like:

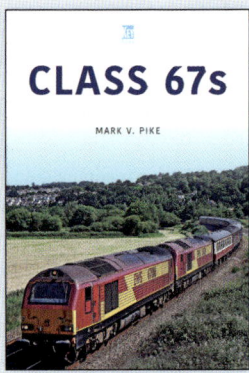

Britain's Railways
Series, Vol. 30

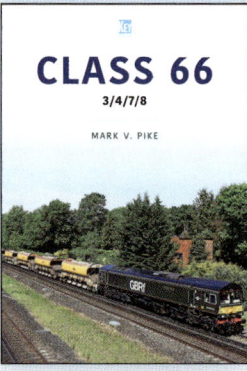

Britain's Railways
Series, Vol. 35

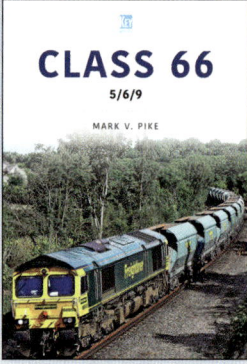

Britain's Railways
Series, Vol. 39

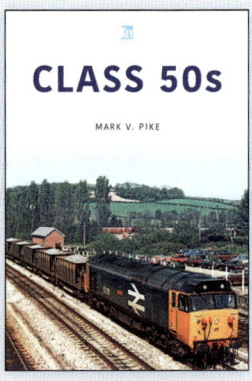

Britain's Railways
Series, Vol. 36

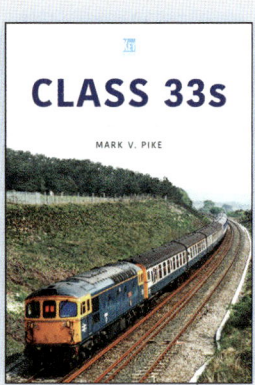

Britain's Railways
Series, Vol. 40

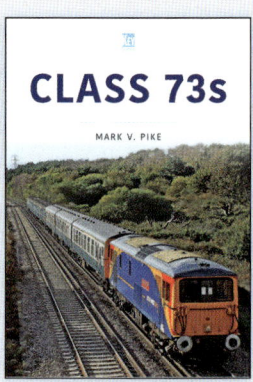

Britain's Railways
Series, Vol. 41

For our full range of titles please visit:
shop.keypublishing.com/books

VIP Book Club

Sign up today and receive
TWO FREE E-BOOKS

Be the first to find out about our forthcoming
book releases and receive exclusive offers.

Register now at **keypublishing.com/vip-book-club**

Our VIP Book Club is a 100% spam-free zone, and we will never share your email with anyone else.
You can read our full privacy policy at: privacy.keypublishing.com